THE Five

MOST IMPORTANT
QUESTIONS
Self-Assessment Tool

THIRD EDITION

PARTICIPANT WORKBOOK

PETER F. DRUCKER

Leader to Leader
INSTITUTE

JOSSEY-BASS
A Wiley Imprint
www.josseybass.com

About the Leader to Leader Institute

Established in 1990 as the Peter F. Drucker Foundation for Nonprofit Management, the Leader to Leader Institute furthers its mission—to strengthen the leadership of the social sector—by providing social sector leaders with essential leadership wisdom, inspiration, and resources to lead for innovation and to build vibrant social sector organizations. It is this essential social sector, in collaboration with its partners in the private and public sectors, that changes lives and builds a society of healthy children, strong families, decent housing, safe neighborhoods, good schools, and work that dignifies, all embraced by the diverse, inclusive, cohesive community that cares about all of its people.

The Leader to Leader Institute strengthens the leadership of the social sector by providing resources and support for

- Managing for the mission

- Making innovation part of strategy

- Developing productive partnerships, collaborations, and alliances

- Facilitating self-assessment

- Promoting and building richly diverse, inclusive organizations and communities

Leader to Leader Institute
320 Park Avenue, 3rd Floor
New York, NY 10022-6839
Telephone: (212) 224-1174
Fax: (212) 224-2508
E-mail: contact@leadertoleader.org, Website: www.leadertoleader.org

Other Publications from the Leader to Leader Institute

The Organization of the Future 2: Visions, Strategies, and Insights on Managing in a New Era, *Frances Hesselbein, Marshall Goldsmith, Editors*

The Five Most Important Questions You Will Ever Ask About Your Organization, *Peter F. Drucker with contributions from Jim Collins, Philip Kotler, Jim Kouzes, Judith Rodin, V. Kasturi Rangan, and Frances Hesselbein*

Leader to Leader 2: Enduring Insights on Leadership from the Leader to Leader Institute's Award-Winning Journal, *Frances Hesselbein, Alan Shrader, Editors*

In Extremis Leadership, *Thomas A. Kolditz*

The Leader of the Future 2, *Frances Hesselbein, Marshall Goldsmith, Editors*

Leadership Lessons from West Point, *Major Doug Crandall, Editor*

Leading Organizational Learning: Harnessing the Power of Knowledge, *Marshall Goldsmith, Howard Morgan, Alexander J. Ogg*

Be*Know*Do: Leadership the Army Way, *Frances Hesselbein, General Eric K. Shinseki, Editors*

Hesselbein on Leadership, *Frances Hesselbein*

Peter F. Drucker: An Intellectual Journey (video), *Leader to Leader Institute*

The Collaboration Challenge, *James E. Austin*

Meeting the Collaboration Challenge Workbook, *The Drucker Foundation*

On Leading Change: A Leader to Leader Guide, *Frances Hesselbein, Rob Johnston, Editors*

On High-Performance Organizations: A Leader to Leader Guide, *Frances Hesselbein, Rob Johnston, Editors*

On Creativity, Innovation, and Renewal: A Leader to Leader Guide, *Frances Hesselbein, Rob Johnston, Editors*

On Mission and Leadership: A Leader to Leader Guide, *Frances Hesselbein, Rob Johnston, Editors*

Leading for Innovation, *Frances Hesselbein, Marshall Goldsmith, Iain Somerville, Editors*

Leading in a Time of Change (video), *Peter F. Drucker, Peter M. Senge, Frances Hesselbein*

Leading in a Time of Change Viewer's Workbook, *Peter F. Drucker, Peter M. Senge, Frances Hesselbein*

Leading Beyond the Walls, *Frances Hesselbein, Marshall Goldsmith, Iain Somerville, Editors*

The Organization of the Future, *Frances Hesselbein, Marshall Goldsmith, Richard Beckhard, Editors*

The Community of the Future, *Frances Hesselbein, Marshall Goldsmith, Richard Beckhard, Richard F. Schubert, Editors*

Leader to Leader: Enduring Insights on Leadership from the Drucker Foundation, *Frances Hesselbein, Paul Cohen, Editors*

Excellence in Nonprofit Leadership (video), *Featuring Peter F. Drucker, Max De Pree, Frances Hesselbein, Michele Hunt; Moderated by Richard F. Schubert*

Excellence in Nonprofit Leadership Workbook and Facilitator's Guide, *Peter F. Drucker Foundation for Nonprofit Management*

Lessons in Leadership (video), *Peter F. Drucker*

Lessons in Leadership Workbook and Facilitator's Guide, *Peter F. Drucker*

The Leader of the Future, *Frances Hesselbein, Marshall Goldsmith, Richard Beckhard, Editors*

Contents

Foreword

"You say we should achieve excellence, but how do we know when we get there?" was the most compelling question the Peter Drucker Foundation, now the Leader to Leader Institute, heard in the fall of 1990, when our work began. This *Self-Assessment Tool,* in its third edition, is our continued response.

Remarkable opportunities exist for those who would lead their enterprises and this country into a new kind of society—of healthy children, strong families, good schools, decent housing, and work that dignifies, all embraced by a cohesive, inclusive community that cares about all its people. In this period of unprecedented worldwide societal transformation, leaders from all sectors will dare to see life and community whole. They will strive to address the needs of body, mind, and spirit. They will view their work as an amazing opportunity to express everything within that gives passion and light to living. They will have the courage to lead from the front on issues, principles, vision, and mission that becomes the star to steer by.

Self-assessment is a discussion about the future and how your organization will shape it. It is an intellectual and emotional adventure—for minds and hearts are involved. Rather than working in isolation, mission-driven social sector organizations, businesses, and government institutions with vision and new mind-sets will forge partnerships across all three sectors—the private, public, and social—to collaborate in building healthy communities. They will welcome the challenge of accountability; define and achieve meaningful results; and articulate their accomplishments in ways that draw interest, energy, and support to their mission. They will *change lives.*

The demand that social sector organizations (in fact, all organizations) show results is not a passing trend. Nor should it be. The demand today and for the future is *performance.* The first requirement of staff, volunteers, socially responsible businesses, and donors at all levels is to ensure that a difference is being made. They are asking, *How are you changing lives and communities for the better?* In this environment, self-assessment is vital.

If Peter Drucker were here to sit down with your organization, he would ask, *What is our mission? Who is our customer? What does the customer value? What are our results?* and *What is our plan?* He would ask these five questions because they go to the very heart of any organization—why it exists and how it will make a difference. They are The Five Most Important Questions because they are the *essential* questions.

One self-assessment participant called the questions "sharply pointed as a bayonet." The questions are not easy. By asking them, you will focus on excellence in performance and what you must do to achieve it. We, board and staff members of the Leader to Leader Institute, periodically ask the questions of ourselves, and we know when *you* ask these questions, all who participate in seeking answers will have an exuberant dialogue and conclusion.

This must be a *three-way* conversation that includes the board, the staff, and the customer. In the self-assessment process, we ask that you go directly to those you serve—your volunteers, your partners, your customers, and your supporters—and let their insights influence your own. How you think about results and how you innovate and change will be immeasurably enriched. When board and staff members, learning from their customers, shape their organization's mission and goals, they create an organizational focus with passion and energy behind it that carries the organization far beyond what one can imagine.

To be able to say "We are successful; we are furthering the mission," a social sector or a socially responsible organization must continuously appraise its performance. This revised and updated edition of the Leader to Leader Institute's *Self-Assessment Tool* is the result of such an appraisal. Since 1993, over 140,000 social sector leaders have purchased the *Self-Assessment Tool* for their organizations. Many leaders in all three sectors have written or spoken with us about their experience with Drucker's self-assessment process.

The feedback we have received is significant. We hear the *Tool* is a success, that using it indeed deepens an organization's sense of purpose and helps to define and achieve results. Our customers have told us they need more guidance in adapting the *Tool* to their particular setting, to streamline the *Participant Workbook,* to underscore the importance of listening to *their* customers, to clarify and sharpen the planning process, and to provide additional insights from Peter Drucker's philosophy on how to successfully implement a plan. And this is what we did. We are deeply grateful for the opportunity to learn from the ideas of those with on-the-ground experience and to respond to our valued customers.

We also have learned of the *Tool*'s great flexibility. It is used by organizations in all three sectors. It is adapted and woven into a range of planning exercises for boards and management teams, project teams, and individuals. The *Tool* serves as a university-level teaching tool. And it is part of the reference libraries of executives in all three sectors. It is used by large and small organizations.

We welcome your use of the *Tool* however it best serves you. Please adapt the self-assessment process to the needs and culture of your organization. *Make it your own.*

The mission of the Leader to Leader Institute is to "strengthen the leadership of the social sector." We have no greater expression of this mission than the *Self-Assessment Tool.* The *Tool* is an adventure in organizational self-discovery, a means for assessing how to *be*—how to develop quality, character, values, and courage. It begins with questions and ends with action. To quote a customer, "It has only one purpose: to put the organization on track. And it works." On behalf of the Leader to Leader Institute, we welcome and encourage you on this journey into the future.

September 2010

Frances Hesselbein
President and Chief Executive Officer
Leader to Leader Institute
(founded as the Peter F. Drucker
Foundation for Nonprofit Management)

About Peter F. Drucker

Peter F. Drucker (1909–2005)—widely considered to be the world's foremost pioneer of management theory—was a writer, teacher, and consultant specializing in strategy and policy for businesses and social sector organizations. Drucker's career as a writer, consultant, and teacher spanned nearly seventy-five years. His groundbreaking work turned modern management theory into a serious discipline. He has influenced or created nearly every facet of its application, including decentralization, privatization, empowerment, and understanding of "the knowledge worker." He is the author of thirty-nine books, which have been translated into more than twenty languages. Thirteen books deal with society, economics, and politics; fifteen deal with management. Two of his books are novels, one is autobiographical, and he is coauthor of a book on Japanese painting. He has made four series of educational films based on his management books. He was an editorial columnist for the *Wall Street Journal* and a frequent contributor to the *Harvard Business Review* and other periodicals.

Drucker was born in 1909 in Vienna and was educated there and in England. He took his doctorate in public and international law while working as a newspaper reporter in Frankfurt, Germany. He then worked as an economist for an international bank in London. Drucker moved to London in 1933 to escape Hitler's Germany and took a job as a securities analyst for an insurance firm. Four years later, he married Doris Schmitz, and the couple departed for the United States in 1937.

Drucker landed a part-time teaching position at Sarah Lawrence College in New York in 1939. He joined the faculty of Bennington College in Vermont as professor of politics and philosophy in 1942, and the next year put his academic career on hold to spend two years studying the management structure of General Motors. This experience led to his book *Concept of the Corporation*, an immediate best-seller in the United States and Japan, which validated the notion that great companies could stand among humankind's noblest inventions. For more than twenty years, he was professor of management at the Graduate Business School of New York University. He was awarded the Presidential Citation, the university's highest honor.

Drucker came to California in 1971, where he was instrumental in the development of the country's first executive MBA program for working professionals at Claremont Graduate University (then known as Claremont Graduate School). The university's management school was named the Peter F. Drucker Graduate School of Management in his honor in 1987. He taught his last class at the school in the spring of 2002. His courses consistently attracted the largest number of students of any other class offered by the university.

As a consultant, Drucker specialized in strategy and policy for governments, businesses, and nonprofit organizations. His special focus was on the organization and work of top management. He worked with some of the world's largest businesses and with small and entrepreneurial companies. In recent years, he worked extensively with nonprofit organizations, including universities, hospitals, and churches. He served as a consultant to a number of agencies of the U.S. government and with the governments of Canada, Japan, Mexico, and other nations throughout the world.

Peter Drucker has been hailed in the United States and abroad as the seminal thinker, writer, and lecturer on the contemporary organization. Drucker's work has had a major influence on modern organizations and their management over the past sixty years. Valued for keen insight and the ability to convey his ideas in popular language, Drucker has often set the agenda in management thinking. Central to his philosophy is the view that people are an organization's most valuable resource and that a manager's job is to prepare and free people to perform. In 1997, he was featured on the cover of *Forbes* magazine under the headline "Still the Youngest Mind," and *BusinessWeek* has called him "the most enduring management thinker of our time." On June 21, 2002, Peter Drucker received the Presidential Medal of Freedom from President George W. Bush.

Drucker received honorary doctorates from numerous universities around the world, including the United States, Belgium, Czechoslovakia, Great Britain, Japan, Spain, and Switzerland. He was honorary chairman of the Leader to Leader Institute from 1990 to 2002. He passed away on November 11, 2005, at age ninety-five.

How to Use This Workbook

Understanding Your Role

The *Self-Assessment Tool* was intentionally developed as a flexible resource. How you use the *Workbook* will depend on your setting and the particular purpose for which self-assessment is being conducted in your organization.

The *Workbook* may be in your hands because you have an interest in The Five Most Important Questions or because you have initiated or been invited by your organization's leadership to take part in self-assessment. You also may be part of a team selected to embark on this journey. Whatever the case, your experience and unique point of view will help your organization become more effective. Make sure that you understand your organization's overall focus of self-assessment and your role in the process. It is the responsibility of your organization's leadership to explain the purpose for self-assessment and to orient you in the process.

Introductory Workshop

If you are or will be attending an introductory workshop, your facilitator or group leader may have distributed the *Workbook* in advance. If you were not instructed to do so already, you are encouraged to read through the *Workbook* and review the worksheets, which you'll be working with in more depth during the workshop. If a facilitator assigned specific readings or worksheets, be sure to allow yourself sufficient time to complete this pre-work and digest the material. Doing so will make the time spent in the workshop or meeting more valuable. Be sure to bring the *Workbook* with you as well.

Prior to a workshop or when considering one, you may also want to read *The Five Most Important Questions You Will Ever Ask About Your Organization* (Jossey-Bass, 2008). This little book will orient you to Peter Drucker's essential questions and it provides insights from Jim Collins, Philip Kotler, Jim Kouzes, Judith Rodin, V. Kasturi Rangan, and Frances Hesselbein on the questions and on Drucker himself. If you are interested in conducting an introductory workshop, the *Facilitator's Guide* contains resources on how to design and lead half-day, full-day, and two-day workshops.

Organizational Self-Assessment

If you have been asked to participate in organizational self-assessment, you are a part of a strategic planning process that will help your organization revisit its mission, determine future direction, and develop a plan to achieve excellence in performance.

To help your organization explore Peter Drucker's Five Most Important Questions, you will use this *Participant Workbook* to (1) guide your individual thinking and (2) prepare for productive dialogue with other leaders in your organization. Dialogue sessions produce results-oriented strategic thinking and decision making.

Each chapter of the *Workbook* contains introductory passages from Peter Drucker, followed by worksheets you will use to explore each of The Five Most Important Questions. The passages are intended to help you understand self-assessment by providing theory, concepts, insight, and pertinent examples. Self-assessment is a framework for appraising performance and determining direction. *It is essential that you explore all of The Five Most Important Questions in the sequence they are presented.* At any point, you may revisit a question you have already examined.

Two copies of each worksheet are provided in this workbook so that if you attend an introductory workshop and write on the first copy, the second will be available should you need it during your self-assessment process.

Preparing for Facilitated Group Dialogue

Once you have familiarized yourself with self-assessment, you are ready to participate in a group discussion led by a facilitator. In group sessions, you will work with others in your organization to help assess its effectiveness and make recommendations for the future.

In a discussion group, there are no right or wrong answers. Participants are encouraged to agree or disagree freely with other members of the group, to change their minds, or to ask each other questions. When appropriate, a summary of the facilitated dialogue—including all areas discussed, agreements reached, decisions made, and next steps—will be compiled by the facilitator and presented to you or your organization's leadership for review. What is learned during self-assessment will be used to revisit the mission, determine direction, and take action.

Plan to spend at least one to two hours familiarizing yourself with the *Workbook* before you join your colleagues in facilitated dialogue. While you should review the worksheets for Question 5—"What Is Our Plan?"—they should not be completed until the organization is ready to revisit the mission, determine goals, and prepare the plan. If your organization selects worksheets for you to complete before your facilitated dialogue, please take enough time to do so. Although the workbook will not be collected, be sure to bring it with you to your group session or sessions, as it will serve as a helpful reference.

Understanding Self-Assessment Terms

This workbook uses Peter Drucker's core leadership and management principles and terminology. It is essential you use the terms during self-assessment—they will help you stay focused on results. Following are terms you will need to be familiar with before using this workbook. A glossary of additional terms can be found on p. 99.

Customer value	That which satisfies customers' needs (physical and psychological well-being), wants (where, when, and how a service or product is provided), and aspirations (desired future results).
Customers	Those who must be satisfied in order for the organization to achieve results. The *primary customer* is the person whose life is changed through the organization's work. *Supporting customers* are volunteers, members, partners, funders, referral sources, staff, and others who must be satisfied in order for the organization to achieve results.
Mission	The organization's reason for being, its purpose. Says what, in the end, the organization wants to be remembered for.
Results	The organization's bottom line. Defined in changed lives—behavior, circumstances, health, hopes, competence, or capacity. Results are always outside the organization.

Self-Assessment

The First Action Requirement of Leadership[1]

Editor's Note: This material and some of the proceeding sections authored by Peter Drucker are from the previous edition of the Participant Workbook. *Although some of the references and terminology are dated, Drucker's points and concepts are as relevant as ever to social sector organizations or to any organization with a socially driven mission.*

A Time to Shape the Future

Nonprofit institutions are central to the quality of life in America and central to citizenship; indeed, they carry the values of American society and the American tradition. The social sector organization has been America's resounding success in the last fifty years, whether we talk of institutions like the American Heart Association, which has taken leadership on major health issues; or of youth services such as the Girl Scouts of the U.S.A.; or of the recovery techniques of Alcoholics Anonymous; or of the fast-growing synagogues, churches, and mosques; or of the community developers that have revitalized urban neighborhoods; or of outstanding museums and colleges; or of the many other nonprofit groups that have emerged as the center of effective social action in a rapidly changing and turbulent America.

We are living through a period of sharp transformation. People born fifty years from now will not be able to imagine the world into which their own grandparents were born. Society is rearranging itself—its worldview, its basic values, its social and political structure, its arts, its key institutions. Social sector organizations will be needed even more urgently in the next decades as needs grow in two areas. First they will grow in what has traditionally been considered *charity*—helping the poor, the disabled, those who suffer deprivation, the victims of violence or disaster. And they will grow, perhaps even faster, in services that aim to *change the community and to change people.*

What new questions will arise and where the big new issues will lie, we can, I believe, already discover with some degree of probability. In many areas we can also describe what will not work. But answers to most questions are still largely hidden in the womb of the future. What the future society will look like depends on leaders in all sectors and on each of us in our work and life. This is a time to *shape the future*—precisely because everything is in flux. This is a time for self-assessment, a time for clear-minded decisions, and, above all, a time for action.

The Search for Community, Commitment, and Contribution

Every other American adult—90 million people all told—works at least three hours a week as "unpaid staff," that is, as a volunteer with a nonprofit organization. By the year 2010, the number of such unpaid staff people should have risen to 120 million, and their average hours of work to five per week. The main reason for this upsurge of volunteer participation in the United States is not the increase in need. The reason is the search for community, for commitment, and for contribution. Again and again when I talk to volunteers, I ask, "Why are you willing to give all this time when you are already working hard?" Again and again I get the same answer, "Because here I know what I am doing. Here I contribute. Here I am part of a community."

The nonprofit organization is a new center of meaningful citizenship, of active commitment. It offers the means to make a difference in one's community, one's society, one's own country, and beyond. Citizenship in and through the social sector is not a panacea for the world's ills, but it may be a prerequisite for tackling these ills. The organizations of the social sector have the critical leadership challenge to restore civic responsibility and the civic pride that is the mark of community.

Focus on Results

All social sector organizations share the common "bottom line" of *changed lives*. This is where *results* are—in the lives of people outside the organization—and achieving these bottom-line results is of absolute importance. Forty-five years ago, when I first began working with nonprofit organizations, many felt that good intentions were enough. "Business" subjects such as management, marketing, and return on investment were almost never discussed. Today, nonprofits have to think through very clearly what results are for their organization. They must demonstrate both commitment *and* competence in a highly demanding environment. People are no longer interested to know, "Is it a good cause?" Instead, they ask, "What is being achieved?

Is this a responsible organization worthy of my investment? What difference is being made in society, in this community, in the life of individuals?" The successful nonprofit institution will hold itself accountable for performance inside the organization—for effective marketing, for exemplary management of human and financial resources, for contribution in all areas—but always with the central focus on its one bottom line: changed lives.

The Five Most Important Questions

When we announced in 1990 that we were establishing the Peter F. Drucker Foundation for Nonprofit Management [now the Leader to Leader Institute], many in the social sector approached me, along with Frances Hesselbein and members of our board, saying, "The most important management resource we need is a method to help us think through what we are doing, why we are doing it, and what we *must* do." And so we developed this *Self-Assessment Tool,* which presents The Five Most Important Questions for any nonprofit organization to ask: *What is our mission? Who is our customer? What does the customer value? What are our results? What is our plan?*

The questions are straightforward—and deceptively simple. Throughout the self-assessment process, you will examine the fundamental question of your mission: what the mission is and what it *should* be. You will determine your *primary customer:* the person whose life is changed through your work. You will determine your *supporting customers:* volunteers, partners, donors, and others you must satisfy. You will engage in research to learn directly from customers what they value, decide what your results should be, and develop a plan with long-range goals and measurable objectives.

Encourage Constructive Dissent

All the first-rate decision makers I've observed had a very simple rule: If you have quick consensus on an important matter, don't make the decision. Acclamation means nobody has done the homework. The organization's decisions are important and risky, and they *should* be controversial. There is a very old saying—it goes back all the way to Aristotle and later became an axiom of the early Christian Church: In essentials unity, in action freedom, and in all things trust. Trust requires that dissent come out in the open.

Nonprofit institutions need a healthy atmosphere for dissent if they wish to foster innovation and commitment. Nonprofits must encourage honest and constructive disagreement precisely because everybody is committed to a good cause: your opinion versus mine can easily be taken as your good faith versus mine. Without proper encouragement, people have a tendency to avoid such difficult, but vital, discussions or turn them into underground feuds.

Another reason to encourage dissent is that any organization needs its nonconformist. This is not the kind of person who says, "There is a right way and a wrong way—and our way." Rather, he or she asks, "What is the right way *for the future?*" and is ready to change. Finally, open discussion uncovers what the objections are. With genuine participation, a decision doesn't need to be sold. Suggestions can be incorporated, objections addressed, and the decision itself becomes a commitment to action.

Creating Tomorrow's Society of Citizens

Your commitment to self-assessment is a commitment to developing yourself and your organization as a leader. You will expand your vision by listening to your customers, by encouraging constructive dissent, by looking at the sweeping transformation taking place in society. You have vital judgments ahead: whether to change the mission, whether to abandon programs that have outlived their usefulness and concentrate resources elsewhere, how to match opportunities with your competence and commitment, *how you will build community and change lives.* Self-assessment is the first action requirement of leadership: the constant resharpening, constant refocusing, never being really satisfied. And the time to do this is when you are successful. If you wait until things start to go down, then it's very difficult.

We are creating tomorrow's society of citizens through the social sector, through *your* nonprofit organization. And in that society, everybody is a leader, everybody is responsible, everybody acts. Therefore, mission and leadership are not just things to read about, to listen to; they are things to *do* something about. Self-assessment can and should convert good intentions and knowledge into effective action—not next year but tomorrow morning.

Peter F. Drucker

Question 1:
What Is Our Mission?

Worksheet 1.1:
What Is Our Current Mission?

Worksheet 1.2:
Does Our Mission Need to Be Revisited?

Worksheet 1.3:
**What Are the Emerging Trends That Will
Have the Greatest Impact?**

Worksheet 1.4:
What Are Our Opportunities?

Question 2:
Who Is Our Customer?

Question 3:
What Does the Customer Value?

Question 4:
What Are Our Results?

Question 5:
What Is Our Plan?

Question 1:
What Is Our Mission?[2]

Each social sector institution exists to make a distinctive difference in the lives of individuals and in society. Making this difference is the mission—the organization's purpose and very reason for being. Each of more than one million nonprofit organizations in the United States may have a very different mission, but changing lives is always the starting point and ending point. A mission cannot be impersonal; it has to have deep meaning, be something you believe in—something you know is right. A fundamental responsibility of leadership is to make sure that everybody knows the mission, understands it, lives it.

Many years ago, I sat down with the administrators of a major hospital to think through the mission of the emergency room. As do most hospital administrators, they began by saying, "Our mission is health care." And that's the wrong definition. The hospital does not take care of health; the hospital takes care of illness. It took us a long time to come up with the very simple and (most people thought) too-obvious statement that the emergency room was there *to give assurance to the afflicted.* To do that well, you had to know what really went on. And, to the surprise of the physicians and nurses, the function of a good emergency room in their community was to tell eight out of ten people there was nothing wrong that a good night's sleep wouldn't fix. "You've been shaken up. Or the baby has the flu. All right, it's got convulsions, but there is nothing seriously wrong with the child." The doctors and nurses gave assurance.

We worked it out, but it sounded awfully obvious. Yet translating the mission into action meant that everybody who came in was seen by a qualified person in less than a minute. The first objective was to see everybody, almost immediately—because that is the only way to give assurance.

It Should Fit on a T-Shirt

The effective mission statement is short and sharply focused. It should fit on a T-shirt. The mission says *why* you do what you do, not the means by which you do it. The mission is broad, even eternal, yet directs you to do the right things now and into the future so that everyone in the organization can say, "What I am doing contributes to the goal." So it must be clear, and it must inspire. Every board member, volunteer, and staff person should be able to see the mission and say, "Yes. This is something I want to be remembered for."

To have an effective mission, you have to work out an exacting match of your opportunities, competence, and commitment. Every good mission statement reflects all three. You look first at the outside environment. The organization that starts from the inside and then tries to find places to put its resources is going to fritter itself away. Above all, it will focus on yesterday. Demographics change. Needs change. You must search out the accomplished facts—things that have already happened—that present challenges and opportunities for the organization. Leadership has no choice but to anticipate the future and attempt to mold it, bearing in mind that whoever is content to rise with the tide will also fall with it. It is not given to mortals to do any of these things well, but, lacking divine guidance, you must still assess where your opportunity lies.

Look at the state of the art, at changing conditions, at competition, the funding environment, at gaps to be filled. The hospital isn't going to sell shoes, and it's not going into education on a big scale. It's going to take care of the sick. But the specific aim may change. Things that are of primary importance now may become secondary or totally irrelevant very soon. With the limited resources you have—and I don't just mean people and money but also competence—where can you dig in and make a difference? Where can you set a new standard of performance? What really inspires your commitment?

Why Does the Organization Exist?

Defining the nonprofit mission is difficult, painful, and risky. But it alone enables you to set goals and objectives and go to work. Unless the mission is explicitly expressed, clearly understood, and supported by every member of the organization, the enterprise is at the mercy of events. Decision makers throughout will decide and act on the basis of different, incompatible, and conflicting ideas. They will pull in opposing directions without even being aware of their divergence, and your performance is what suffers. Common vision, understanding, and unity of direction and effort of the entire organization depend on defining the mission and what the mission *should* be.

Refining the Mission Statement[3]

Every three to five years, you should look at the mission again to decide whether it needs to be refocused because the demographics of your customers have changed, because you should abandon something that produces no results or needs resources beyond the organization's competencies, or because the objective has been accomplished.

You must think through priorities. That's easy to say, but to act on it is very hard because doing so always involves abandoning things that may look attractive, or giving up programs that people both inside and outside the organization are strongly encouraging you to keep. But if you don't concentrate your institution's resources, you are not going to get results. This may be the ultimate test of leadership: the ability to think through the priority decision and to make it stick.

Make Principled Decisions[4]

One cautionary note: *never subordinate the mission in order to get money.* If there are opportunities that threaten the integrity of the organization, you must say no. Otherwise, you sell your soul. I sat in on a discussion at a museum that had been offered a donation of important art on conditions that no self-respecting museum could possibly accept. Yet a few board members said, "Let's take the donation. We can change the conditions down the road." "No, that's unconscionable!" others responded, and the board fought over the issue. They finally agreed they would lose too much by compromising basic principles to please a donor. The board forfeited some very nice pieces of sculpture, but core values had to come first.

Keep Thinking It Through

Keep the central question, What is our mission? in front of you throughout the self-assessment process. Step by step you will analyze challenges and opportunities, identify your customers, learn what they value, and define your results. When it is time to develop the plan, you will take all that you have learned and revisit the mission to affirm or change it.

As you begin, consider this wonderful sentence from a sermon of that great poet and religious philosopher of the seventeenth century, John Donne: "Never start with tomorrow to reach eternity. Eternity is not being reached by small steps." We start with the long range and then feed back and say, "What do we do *today?*" The ultimate test is not the beauty of the mission statement. The ultimate test is your performance.

Peter F. Drucker

Worksheet 1.1:
What Is Our Current Mission?
(Workshop)

a. Write or attach a copy of the organization's mission statement here.

b. What is our organization's reason for being? Why do we do what we do?

c. What, in the end, do we want to be remembered for?

Worksheet 1.1:
What Is Our Current Mission?
(Organizational)

a. Write or attach a copy of the organization's mission statement here.

b. What is our organization's reason for being? Why do we do what we do?

c. What, in the end, do we want to be remembered for?

Worksheet 1.2:
Does Our Mission Need to Be Revisited?
(Workshop)

a. Rate the current mission using the following criteria and then decide if it should be revisited.

The Mission	Yes	To Some Extent	Not at All
Is short and focused—fits on a T-shirt	☐	☐	☐
Is clear and easily understood	☐	☐	☐
Defines purpose—why we do what we do, our reason for being	☐	☐	☐
Does not prescribe means	☐	☐	☐
Is sufficiently broad	☐	☐	☐
Inspires our commitment	☐	☐	☐
Says what, in the end, we want to be remembered for	☐	☐	☐

b. Should the mission be revisited?   ☐ Yes   ☐ No

If so, what changes should we consider?

Worksheet 1.2:
Does Our Mission Need to Be Revisited?
(Organizational)

a. Rate the current mission using the following criteria and then decide if it should be revisited.

The Mission	Yes	To Some Extent	Not at All
Is short and focused—fits on a T-shirt	☐	☐	☐
Is clear and easily understood	☐	☐	☐
Defines purpose—why we do what we do, our reason for being	☐	☐	☐
Does not prescribe means	☐	☐	☐
Is sufficiently broad	☐	☐	☐
Inspires our commitment	☐	☐	☐
Says what, in the end, we want to be remembered for	☐	☐	☐

b. Should the mission be revisited?   ☐ Yes   ☐ No

If so, what changes should we consider?

Worksheet 1.3:
What Are the Emerging Trends That Will Have the Greatest Impact?
(Workshop)

a. Identify emerging trends that will impact the organization. Describe the trend and note the data sources used to identify it (environmental scan, internal data, experience, and insight). Indicate if the trends will affect the organization in the short term, the long term, or both.*

Describe Trends	Note Data Sources
Changing demographics? ☐ Short Term ☐ Long Term	
Changing community conditions? ☐ Short Term ☐ Long Term	
Cultural or social trends? ☐ Short Term ☐ Long Term	

* *Short term* often is designated as one year; *long term* as three to five years.

Describe Trends   **Note Data Sources**

Economic trends; changes in the funding environment?
☐ Short Term   ☐ Long Term

Politics, legislation, or regulation?
☐ Short Term   ☐ Long Term

Media and communications?
☐ Short Term   ☐ Long Term

* *Short term* often is designated as one year; *long term* as three to five years.

The Five Most Important Questions Self-Assessment Tool, Participant Workbook, Third Edition. Copyright © 2010 by Leader to Leader Institute. Reproduced by permission of Jossey-Bass, an Imprint of Wiley.

Describe Trends	**Note Data Sources**

New models, methods, and technologies?
    ☐ Short Term   ☐ Long Term

Competition?
    ☐ Short Term   ☐ Long Term

Other?
    ☐ Short Term   ☐ Long Term

* *Short term* often is designated as one year; *long term* as three to five years.

Worksheet 1.3:
What Are the Emerging Trends That Will Have the Greatest Impact? (cont'd) (Workshop)

b. What are the three to five trends that will have the greatest impact on our organization?

1.

2.

3.

4.

5.

a. Identify emerging trends that will impact the organization. Describe the trend and note the data sources used to identify it (environmental scan, internal data, experience, and insight). Indicate if the trends will affect the organization in the short term, the long term, or both.*

Describe Trends	Note Data Sources

Changing demographics?
☐ Short Term   ☐ Long Term

Changing community conditions?
☐ Short Term   ☐ Long Term

Cultural or social trends?
☐ Short Term   ☐ Long Term

* *Short term* often is designated as one year; *long term* as three to five years.

Describe Trends   **Note Data Sources**

Economic trends; changes in the funding environment?
☐ Short Term   ☐ Long Term

Politics, legislation, or regulation?
☐ Short Term   ☐ Long Term

Media and communications?
☐ Short Term   ☐ Long Term

* *Short term* often is designated as one year; *long term* as three to five years.

Describe Trends	Note Data Sources

New models, methods, and technologies?
☐ Short Term   ☐ Long Term

Competition?
☐ Short Term   ☐ Long Term

Other?
☐ Short Term   ☐ Long Term

* *Short term* often is designated as one year; *long term* as three to five years.

---

b. What are the three to five trends that will have the greatest impact on our organization?

1.

2.

3.

4.

5.

Worksheet 1.4:
What Are Our Opportunities?
(Workshop)

a. Refer to Worksheet 1.3, as well as other data sources (environmental scan, internal data, experience, and insight) to identify the organization's opportunities. Indicate if they are available in the short term, the long term, or both.*

---

1. What opportunities does the organization have to address compelling issues or conditions?

☐ Short Term
☐ Long Term

---

2. What opportunities does the organization have to fill a gap in its area of service?

☐ Short Term
☐ Long Term

---

3. What opportunities does the organization have to be a leader, to set a new standard of performance?

☐ Short Term
☐ Long Term

---

* Short term often is designated as one year; long term as three to five years.

---

4. What opportunities does the organization have to meet the interests of potential partners or funders?

☐ Short Term
☐ Long Term

5. Other opportunities:

☐ Short Term
☐ Long Term

* *Short term* often is designated as one year; *long term* as three to five years.

b. Which opportunities are the most promising for the organization? Why?

Worksheet 1.4:
What Are Our Opportunities?
(Organizational)

a. Refer to Worksheet 1.3, as well as other data sources (environmental scan, internal data, experience, and insight) to identify the organization's opportunities. Indicate if they are available in the short term, the long term, or both.*

1. What opportunities does the organization have to address compelling issues or conditions?

☐ Short Term
☐ Long Term

2. What opportunities does the organization have to fill a gap in its area of service?

☐ Short Term
☐ Long Term

3. What opportunities does the organization have to be a leader, to set a new standard of performance?

☐ Short Term
☐ Long Term

Short term often is designated as one year; *long term* as three to five years.

Worksheet 1.4: What Are Our Opportunities? (cont'd) (Organizational)

---

4. What opportunities does the organization have to meet the interests of potential partners or funders?

☐ Short Term
☐ Long Term

---

5. Other opportunities:

☐ Short Term
☐ Long Term

* *Short term* often is designated as one year; *long term* as three to five years.

b. Which opportunities are the most promising for the organization? Why?

Question 1:
What Is Our Mission?

Question 2:
Who Is Our Customer?

Worksheet 2.1:
Who Are Our Primary and
Supporting Customers?

Worksheet 2.2:
How Will Our Customers Change?

Worksheet 2.3:
Are We Serving the Right Customers?

Question 3:
What Does the
Customer Value?

Question 4:
What Are Our Results?

Question 5:
What Is Our Plan?

Question 2
Who Is Our Customer?[5]

Not long ago, the word *customer* was rarely heard in the social sector. Nonprofit leaders would say, "We don't have customers. That's a marketing term. We have clients . . . recipients . . . patients. We have audience members. We have students." Rather than debate language, I ask, "Who must be satisfied for the organization to achieve results?" When you answer this question, you define your customer as one who values your service, who wants what you offer, who feels it's important to *them.*

Social sector organizations have two types of customers. The *primary customer* is the person whose life is changed through your work. Effectiveness requires focus, and that means *one* response to the question, Who is our primary customer? Those who chase off in too many directions suffer by diffusing their energies and diminishing their performance. *Supporting customers* are volunteers, members, partners, funders, referral sources, employees, and others who must be satisfied. They are all people who can say no, people who have the choice to accept or reject what you offer. You might satisfy them by providing the opportunity for meaningful service, by directing contributions toward results you both believe in, by joining forces to meet community needs.

The primary customer is never the *only* customer, and to satisfy one customer without satisfying the others means there is no performance. This makes it very tempting to say there is more than one primary customer, but effective organizations resist this temptation and keep to a focus—the primary customer.

Identify the Primary Customer

Let me give you a positive example of identifying and concentrating on the primary customer in a complex setting. A mid-sized nonprofit organization's mission is *to increase people's economic and social independence.* They have twenty-five programs considered to be in four different fields, but for thirty-five years they have focused on only one primary customer: *the person with multiple barriers to employment.* In the beginning, this meant the physically handicapped. Today, it still means people with disabilities but also single mothers who want to be finished with welfare, older workers who have been laid off, people with chronic and persistent mental illness living in the community, and those struggling against long-term chemical dependency. Each belongs to a single primary customer group: the person with multiple barriers to employment. Results are measured in every program by whether the customer can now gain and keep productive work.

The primary customer is not necessarily someone you can reach, someone you can sit down with and talk to directly. Primary customers may be infants, or endangered species, or members of a future generation. Whether or not you can have an active dialogue, identifying the primary customer puts your priorities in order and gives you a reference point for critical decisions on the organization's values.

Identify Supporting Customers

The Girl Scouts of the U.S.A. is the largest girls' and women's organization in the world and a nonprofit that exemplifies service to one primary customer—the girl—balanced with satisfaction of many supporting customers, all of whom change over time. A long-held Girl Scouts priority is offering equal access to every girl in the United States. This has not changed since 1912, when the Girl Scouts founder said, "I have something for all the girls." Frances Hesselbein, at the time she was national executive director (1976–1990), told me, "We look at the projections and understand that by the year 2000, one-third of this country will be members of minority groups. Many people are very apprehensive about the future and what this new racial and ethnic composition will mean. We see it as an unprecedented opportunity to reach all girls with a program that will help them in their growing-up years, which are more difficult than ever before."

Reaching a changing primary customer means a new view of supporting customers. Frances explained, "In a housing project with no Girl Scout troop there are hundreds of young girls really needing this kind of program, and families wanting something better for their children. It is important as we reach out to girls in every racial and economic group to understand the very special needs, the culture, the readiness of each group. We work with many supporting customers; with the clergy perhaps, with the director of that housing project, with parents—a group of people from that particular community. We recruit leaders, train them right there. We have to demonstrate our respect for that community, our interest in it. Parents have to know it will be a positive experience for their daughters."

Know Your Customers

Customers are never static. There will be greater or lesser numbers in the groups you already serve. They will become more diverse. Their needs, wants, and aspirations will evolve. There may be entirely new customers you must satisfy to achieve results—individuals who really need the service, want the service, but not in the way in which it is available today. And there are customers you should *stop* serving because the organization has filled a need, because people can be better served elsewhere, or because you are not producing results.

Answering the question, Who is our customer? provides the basis for determining what customers value, defining your results, and developing the plan. Yet, even after careful thought, customers may surprise you; then you must be prepared to adjust. I remember one of my pastoral friends saying of a new program, "Great, a wonderful program for the newly married." The program was indeed a success. But to the consternation of the young assistant pastor who designed it and ran it, not a single newly married couple enrolled. All the participants were young people living together and wondering whether they should get married. And the senior pastor had a terrible time with his brilliant young assistant, who became righteous and said, "We haven't designed it for them!" He wanted to throw them out.

Often, the customer is one step ahead of you. So you must *know your customer*—or quickly get to know them. Time and again you will have to ask, "Who is our customer?" because customers constantly change. The organization that is devoted to results—always with regard for its basic integrity—will adapt and change as they do.

Peter F. Drucker

a. *Who is our primary customer?* The primary customer is the person whose life is changed through the organization's work.

b. *Who are our supporting customers?* Identify who, in addition to the primary customer, must be satisfied in order for the organization to achieve results.

a. *Who is our primary customer?* The primary customer is the person whose life is changed through the organization's work.

b. *Who are our supporting customers?* Identify who, in addition to the primary customer, must be satisfied in order for the organization to achieve results.

Worksheet 2.2:
How Will Our Customers Change?
(Workshop)

Think about how the organization's customers will change for each of the following characteristics. Indicate if the customer will change and briefly describe the anticipated change.

a. How will our *primary customer* change in the next three to five years?

Number: (greater or fewer)   ☐ Yes   ☐ No

Demographics: (age, race, and so on)   ☐ Yes   ☐ No

Needs, wants, and aspirations: ☐ Yes   ☐ No

Other: ☐ Yes   ☐ No

b. What are the implications of these changes for our organization?

c. How will our *supporting customers* change in the next three to five years? For each supporting customer identified in Worksheet 2.1, identify and describe anticipated changes. If necessary, make duplicates of this worksheet for each supporting customer.

Supporting Customer:

Number: (greater or fewer) ☐ Yes ☐ No

Demographics: (age, race, and so on) ☐ Yes ☐ No

Needs, wants, and aspirations: ☐ Yes ☐ No

Other: ☐ Yes ☐ No

d. What are the implications of these changes for our organization?

Worksheet 2.2:
How Will Our Customers Change?
(Organizational)

Think about how the organization's customers will change for each of the following characteristics. Indicate if the customer will change and briefly describe the anticipated change.

a. How will our *primary customer* change in the next three to five years?

Number: (greater or fewer)   ☐ Yes   ☐ No

Demographics: (age, race, and so on)   ☐ Yes   ☐ No

Needs, wants, and aspirations: ☐ Yes   ☐ No

Other: ☐ Yes   ☐ No

b. What are the implications of these changes for our organization?

---

c. How will our *supporting customers* change in the next three to five years? For each supporting customer identified in Worksheet 2.1, identify and describe anticipated changes. If necessary, make duplicates of this worksheet for each supporting customer.

Supporting Customer:

Number: (greater or fewer) ☐ Yes ☐ No

Demographics: (age, race, and so on) ☐ Yes ☐ No

Needs, wants, and aspirations: ☐ Yes ☐ No

Other: ☐ Yes ☐ No

d. What are the implications of these changes for our organization?

Worksheet 2.3:
Are We Serving the Right Customers?
(Workshop)

a. Are there potential new customers we must satisfy to further the mission?

☐ Yes ☐ No

b. If so, who are they? Why should the organization start serving them?

c. Are there existing customers we should stop serving because the organization has satisfied a need, those customers can be better served elsewhere, or we are not producing results?

☐ Yes ☐ No

d. If so, who are they? Why should the organization stop serving them?

Worksheet 2.3:
Are We Serving the Right Customers?
(Organizational)

a. Are there potential new customers we must satisfy to further the mission?

□ Yes   □ No

b. If so, who are they? Why should the organization start serving them?

c. Are there existing customers we should stop serving because the organization has satisfied a need, those customers can be better served elsewhere, or we are not producing results?

□ Yes   □ No

d. If so, who are they? Why should the organization stop serving them?

Question 1:
What Is Our Mission?

Question 2:
Who Is Our Customer?

Question 3:
What Does the
Customer Value?

Worksheet 3.1:
What Do Our Customers Value?

Worksheet 3.2:
What Knowledge Do We Need
to Gain from Our Customers?

Worksheet 3.3:
How Will We Gather Information?

Question 4:
What Are Our Results?

Question 5:
What Is Our Plan?

Question 3:
What Does the Customer Value?[6]

The question, What do customers value?—what satisfies their needs, wants, and aspirations—is so complicated that it can only be answered by customers themselves. And the first rule is that there are no irrational customers. Almost without exception, customers behave rationally in terms of their own realities and their own situation. Leadership should not even try to guess at the answers but should always go to the customers in a systematic quest for those answers. I practice this. Each year I personally telephone a random sample of fifty or sixty students who graduated ten years earlier. I ask, "Looking back, what did we contribute in this school? What is still important to you? What should we do better? What should we stop doing?" And believe me, the knowledge I have gained has had a profound influence.

What does the customer value? may be the most important question. Yet it is the one least often asked. Nonprofit leaders tend to answer it for themselves. "It's the quality of our programs. It's the way we improve the community." People are so convinced they are doing the right things and so committed to their cause that they come to see the institution as an end in itself. But that's a bureaucracy. Instead of asking, "Does it deliver value to our customers?" they ask, "Does it fit our rules?" And that not only inhibits performance but also destroys vision and dedication.

Understand Your Assumptions

My friend Philip Kotler, a professor at Northwestern University, points out that many organizations are very clear about the value they would like to deliver, but they often don't understand that value from the perspective of their customers. They make assumptions based on their own interpretation. So begin with assumptions and find out what *you* believe your customers value. Then you can compare these beliefs with what customers actually are saying, find the differences, and go on to assess your results.

What Does the Primary Customer Value?

Learning what their primary customers value led to significant change in a homeless shelter. The shelter's existing beliefs about value added up to nutritious meals and clean beds. A series of face-to-face interviews with their homeless customers was arranged, and both board and staff members took part. They found out that yes, the food and beds are appreciated but do little or nothing to satisfy the deep aspiration *not to be homeless.* The customers said, "We need a place of safety from which to rebuild our lives, a place we can at least temporarily call a real home." The organization threw out their assumptions and their old rules. They said, "How can we make this shelter a safe haven?" They eliminated the fear that comes with being turned back on the street each morning. They now make it possible to stay at the shelter quite a while, and work with individuals to find out what a rebuilt life means to them and how they can be helped to realize their goal.

The new arrangement also requires more of the customer. Before, it was enough to show up hungry. Now, to get what the customer values most, he must make a commitment. He must work on his problems and plans in order to stay on. The customer's stake in the relationship is greater, as are the organization's results.

What Do Supporting Customers Value?

Your knowledge of what primary customers value is of utmost importance. Yet the reality is, unless you understand equally what supporting customers value, you will not be able to put all the necessary pieces in place for the organization to perform. In social sector organizations there have always been a multitude of supporting customers, in some cases each with a veto power. A school principal has to satisfy teachers, the school board, community partners, the taxpayers, parents, and above all, the primary customer—the young student. The principal has six constituencies, each of which sees the school differently. Each of them is essential, each defines value differently, and each has to be satisfied at least to the point where they don't fire the principal, go on strike, or rebel.

What Will Encourage Contributors?

Knowing what supporting customers value enables nonprofit institutions to address two of today's biggest challenges. The first is to convert individuals who give money into "contributors," that is, citizens who take responsibility, neighbors who care.

Philip Kotler reminds us that this requires careful identification of the appropriate sources of funds and the giving motives. What are that individual's personal reasons for giving money? To whom does he or she give? What results prompt the contributor to say, "Yes, that's what should be done. That's what deserves more of my support"? What does this customer value enough to do more, to really become a partner in furthering the mission?

What Does "Making a Difference" Mean to Each Volunteer?

Then there is the second major challenge for nonprofits: to enhance community and common purpose. What nonprofits do for their volunteers may well be as important as what they do for their primary customers. The reason is that volunteers search for opportunities to make a meaningful contribution. They feel the need to do something where "I can make a difference." But again, you must discover what "making a difference" means to each volunteer and how they must be satisfied in order for them to give their commitment.

Listen to Your Customers

To formulate a successful plan you will need to understand each of your constituencies' concerns, especially what they consider results in the long term. Integrating what customers value into the institution's plan is almost an architectural process, a structural process. It's not too difficult to do once it's understood, but it's hard work. First, think through what knowledge you need to gain. Then listen to customers, accept what they value as objective fact, and make sure the customer's voice is part of your discussions and decisions, not just during this self-assessment process, but continually.

Peter F. Drucker

This worksheet focuses on the existing data the organization uses to understand what the customer values. Worksheets 3.2 and 3.3 focus on the data the organization needs to gather—and how to gather it.

a. Describe what the *primary customer* values (that which satisfies customer needs, wants, and aspirations). Indicate the data sources for each point listed: environmental scan, customer research, experience, and insight.

What does the customer value?	Note Data Sources
Primary customer:	

b. Describe what each *supporting customer* values. Indicate the data sources: environmental scan, customer research, experience, and insight. If necessary, make duplicates of this worksheet for each supporting customer.

What does the customer value?	Note Data Sources
Supporting customer:	
Supporting customer:	

c. Describe what each *potential new customer* values. Indicate the data sources: environmental scan, customer research, experience, and insight. If necessary, make duplicates of this worksheet for each potential new customer.

What does the customer value?	Note Data Sources
Potential new customer:	
Potential new customer:	

This worksheet focuses on the existing data the organization uses to understand what the customer values. Worksheets 3.2 and 3.3 focus on the data the organization needs to gather—and how to gather it.

a. Describe what the *primary customer* values (that which satisfies customer needs, wants, and aspirations). Indicate the data sources for each point listed: environmental scan, customer research, experience, and insight.

What does the customer value?	Note Data Sources
Primary customer:	

b. Describe what each *supporting customer* values. Indicate the data sources: environmental scan, customer research, experience, and insight. If necessary, make duplicates of this worksheet for each supporting customer.

What does the customer value?   **Note Data Sources**

Supporting customer:

Supporting customer:

c. Describe what each *potential new customer* values. Indicate the data sources: environmental scan, customer research, experience, and insight. If necessary, make duplicates of this worksheet for each potential new customer.

What does the customer value?	Note Data Sources
Potential new customer:	
Potential new customer:	

Worksheet 3.2:
What Knowledge Do We Need to Gain from Our Customers?
(Workshop)

Listening to the customer is indispensable. The organization's understanding about its customers may be confirmed or significantly altered when it listens to the customer. Imagine the organization has the opportunity to ask its customers any question. What knowledge is needed to understand what the customer values?

Customer	Knowledge We Need
Primary customer:	

Customer	Knowledge We Need

Supporting customers:

1.

2.

3.

4.

Other:

Worksheet 3.2:
What Knowledge Do We Need to
Gain from Our Customers? (cont'd)
(Workshop)

Customer	Knowledge We Need
Potential new customers:	

1.

2.

3.

Worksheet 3.2:
What Knowledge Do We Need to
Gain from Our Customers?
(Organizational)

Listening to the customer is indispensable. The organization's understanding about its customers may be confirmed or significantly altered when it listens to the customer. Imagine the organization has the opportunity to ask its customers any question. What knowledge is needed to understand what the customer values?

Customer	Knowledge We Need
Primary customer:	

Customer	Knowledge We Need
Supporting customers:	
1.	
2.	
3.	
4.	
Other:	

Customer	Knowledge We Need
Potential new customers:	
1.	
2.	
3.	

Worksheet 3.3:
How Will We Gather Information?
(Workshop)

Use Worksheet 3.2 and identify the best ways to collect the knowledge the organization needs to understand what its customers value. Methods may include customer surveys, focus groups, interviews, and feedback instruments.

Knowledge We Need	Data-Collection Method(s)
1.	
2.	
3.	
4.	
5.	

Worksheet 3.3:
How Will We Gather Information?
(Organizational)

Use Worksheet 3.2 and identify the best ways to collect the knowledge the organization needs to understand what its customers value. Methods may include customer surveys, focus groups, interviews, and feedback instruments.

Knowledge We Need	Data-Collection Method(s)
1.	
2.	
3.	
4.	
5.	

The Five Most Important Questions Self-Assessment Tool, Participant Workbook, Third Edition. Copyright © 2010 by Leader to Leader Institute. Reproduced by permission of Jossey-Bass, an Imprint of Wiley.

Question 1:
What Is Our Mission?

Question 2:
Who Is Our Customer?

Question 3:
What Does the
Customer Value?

Question 4:
What Are Our Results?

Worksheet 4.1:
How Do We Define Results?

Worksheet 4.2:
How Do We Measure Results?

Worksheet 4.3:
How Can We Improve Our Performance?

Question 5:
What Is Our Plan?

Question 4:
What Are Our Results?[7]

The results of social sector organizations are always measured *outside* the organization in changed lives and changed conditions—in people's behavior, circumstances, health, hopes, and, above all, their competence and capacity. To further the mission, each nonprofit needs to determine what should be appraised and judged, then concentrate resources for results.

Look at Short-Term Accomplishments and Long-Term Change

A small mental health center was founded and directed by a dedicated husband-and-wife team, both psychotherapists. They called it a "healing community," and in the fifteen years they ran the organization, they achieved results others had dismissed as impossible. Their primary customers were people diagnosed with schizophrenia, and most came to the center following failure after failure in treatment, their situation nearly hopeless.

The people at the center said, "There *is* somewhere to turn." Their first measure was whether primary customers and their families were willing to try again. The staff had a number of ways to monitor progress. Did participants regularly attend group sessions and participate fully in daily routines? Did the incidence and length of psychiatric hospitalizations decrease? Could these individuals show new understanding of their disease by saying, "I have had an episode," as opposed to citing demons in the closet? As they progressed, could participants set realistic goals for their own next steps?

The center's mission was *to enable people with serious and persistent mental illness to recover,* and after two or more years of intensive work, many could function in this world—they were no longer "incurable." Some were able to return to a life with their family. Others could hold steady jobs. A few completed graduate school. Whether or not members of that healing community did recover—whether the lives of primary customers changed in this fundamental way—was the organization's single bottom line.

In business, you can debate whether profit is really an adequate measuring stick, but without it, there is no business in the long term. In the social sector, no such universal standard for success exists. Each organization must identify its customers, learn what they value, develop meaningful measures, and honestly judge whether, in fact, lives are being changed. This is a new discipline for many nonprofit groups, but it is one that can be learned.

How *Should* the Organization Define Results?

What should be measured and monitored? What are the meaningful criteria for us? What are the prerequisites for success? These are the questions most often raised when I work with social sector organizations to define results. To decide, you return to the mission. You take into account your capabilities, the environment in which you work, the best studies and examples in your field. You listen carefully to primary customers and apply your knowledge of who they are and what they value. You think qualitatively and quantitatively. You work through this discipline until you are resolved on the bottom line and can therefore determine what in your organization must be appraised and judged.

Table 1 shows three examples of decisions on what results should be.

TABLE 1. EXAMPLES OF RESULTS.

Mission: To prevent the spread of AIDS	*Results:* 1. Attitude shifts from "AIDS is something that happens to other people" to acceptance of personal responsibility. 2. People in targeted population groups change their sexual behavior. 3. The number of new cases of AIDS drops.
Mission (for a school): To develop contributing citizens	*Results:* 1. Students are constructive team members and respectful in peer relationships. 2. Graduates go on to advanced education or make a smooth transition to employment. 3. Graduates are active citizens who make a difference in their communities or beyond.

Mission (for a United Way): To improve lives by mobilizing the caring power of communities around the world to advance the common good *Note:* taken from United Way website, http://www.liveunited.org/about/missvis.cfm	*Results:* 1. The most vulnerable are safe and supported. 2. Human services are well resourced and co-operatively strengthen communities, families, and individuals. 3. Economic and social disparities are reduced. 4. Priority community problems and issues are identified and overcome.

Qualitative and Quantitative Measures

Progress and achievement can be appraised in *qualitative* and *quantitative* terms. These two types of measures are interwoven—they shed light on one another—and both are necessary to illuminate in what ways and to what extent lives are being changed.

Qualitative measures address the depth and breadth of change within its particular context. They begin with specific observations, build toward patterns, and tell a subtle, individualized story. Qualitative appraisal offers valid, "rich" data. The education director at a major museum tells of the man who sought her out to explain how the museum had opened his teenage mind to new possibilities in a way he knew literally saved his life. She used this result to support her inspiration for a new initiative with troubled youth. The people in a successful research institute cannot quantify the value of their research ahead of time. But they can sit down every three years and ask, "What have we achieved that contributed to changed lives? Where do we focus now for results tomorrow?" Qualitative results can be in the realm of the intangible, such as instilling hope in a patient battling cancer. Qualitative data, although sometimes more subjective and difficult to grasp, are just as real, just as important, and can be gathered just as systematically as the quantitative.

Quantitative measures use definitive standards. They begin with categories and expectations and tell an objective story. Quantitative appraisal offers valid "hard" data. Examples of quantitative measures are as follows: whether overall school performance improves when at-risk youth have intensive arts education; whether the percentage of welfare recipients who complete training and become employed at a livable wage goes up; whether health professionals change their practice based on new research; whether the number of teenagers who smoke goes up or down; whether incidences of child abuse fall when twenty-four-hour crisis care is available.

Quantitative measures are essential for assessing whether resources are properly concentrated for results, whether progress is being made, whether lives and communities are changing for the better.

Concentrate Resources for Success

Success is realized through concentration, not by splintering. That enormous organization the Salvation Army concentrates on only four or five programs. Its executives have the courage to say, "This is not for us. Other people do it better" or "This is not where we can make the greatest contribution. It does not really fit the strength we have." Success is judged, for example, by the percentage of alcoholics restored to mental and physical health, the number of offenders who stay out of prison, how quickly and completely food kitchens and temporary shelters provide relief at the scene of a disaster.

The most exciting thing to me in almost fifty years of work with nonprofit organizations is that we no longer talk of the *need* but of success in achieving results. To believe that whatever we do is a moral cause and should be pursued whether there is success or not is a perennial temptation for nonprofit executives—and even more for their boards. Everything is "the Lord's work" or "a good cause," but we cannot afford to continue where we seem unable to further the mission. There are exceptions—those who labor in the wilderness, the true believers who are devoted to a cause and to whom success, failure, and results are irrelevant. We need such people. They are our conscience. But very few of them achieve. Nonprofit organizations are asking, "Have we been successful?" and it's high time they did.

Assess What Must Be Strengthened or Abandoned

One of the most important questions for nonprofit leadership is, Do we produce results that are sufficiently outstanding for us to justify putting our resources in this area? Need alone does not justify continuing. Nor does tradition. You must match your mission, your concentration, and your results. Like the New Testament parable of the talents, your job is to invest your resources where the returns are manifold, where you can have success.

To abandon anything is always bitterly resisted. People in any organization are always attached to the obsolete—the things that should have worked but did not, the things that once were productive and no longer are. They are most attached to what in an earlier book (*Managing for Results,* 1964) I called "investments in managerial ego." Yet abandonment comes first. Until that has been accomplished, little else gets done. The acrimonious and emotional debate over what to abandon holds everybody in its grip. Abandoning anything is thus difficult, but only for a fairly short spell. Rebirth can begin once the dead are buried; six months later, everybody wonders, "Why did it take us so long?"

Leadership Is Accountable

If essential performance areas are weak, they must be strengthened. But even then, you must consider "the unthinkable." In one international nonprofit I know of, a highly successful training program had, over thirty years, made a profound difference in health care practices for an entire nation. With an elaborate trans-Pacific infrastructure in place—and a handsome but overly specific endowment supporting it—today's leadership had to address the fact that the training strategy could no longer make a difference for the future and to begin dismantling it in favor of unproved innovations.

There are times to face the fact that the organization as a whole is not performing—that there are weak results everywhere and little prospect of improving. It may be time to merge or to liquidate and put your energies somewhere else. And in some performance areas, whether to strengthen or abandon is not clear. You will need a systematic analysis as part of your plan.

At this point in the self-assessment process, you determine what results for the organization should be and where to concentrate for future success. The mission defines the scope of your responsibility. Leadership is accountable to determine what must be appraised and judged, to protect the organization from squandering resources, and to ensure meaningful results.

Peter F. Drucker

Worksheet 4.1:
How Do We Define Results?
(Workshop)

Results are measured *outside* the organization in the form of changed lives. After exploring the first three questions on mission, customer, and value, how do we define results?

Result:

Result:

Result:

Result:

Worksheet 4.1:
How Do We Define Results?
(Organizational)

Results are measured *outside* the organization in the form of changed lives. After exploring the first three questions on mission, customer, and value, how do we define results?

Result:

Result:

Result:

Result:

Worksheet 4.2:
How Do We Measure Results?
(Workshop)

How do we measure our progress and achievement for each result we identified in Worksheet 4.1?

	Quantitative Measures	Qualitative Measures
Result:		
Result:		
Result:		
Result:		

Worksheet 4.2:
How Do We Measure Results?
(Organizational)

How do we measure our progress and achievement for each result we identified in Worksheet 4.1?

	Quantitative Measures	Qualitative Measures
Result:		
Result:		
Result:		
Result:		

a. How do we concentrate our efforts? List each of the organization's programs and identify if it is strong and can produce greater results; if it is weak and in need of improvement; or if it is a candidate for planned abandonment. Explain why.

Programs

1. ☐ Strong/Growth Area
   ☐ Weak/Needs Improvement
   ☐ Abandon

2. ☐ Strong/Growth Area
   ☐ Weak/Needs Improvement
   ☐ Abandon

3. ☐ Strong/Growth Area
   ☐ Weak/Needs Improvement
   ☐ Abandon

4. ☐ Strong/Growth Area
   ☐ Weak/Needs Improvement
   ☐ Abandon

5. ☐ Strong/Growth Area
   ☐ Weak/Needs Improvement
   ☐ Abandon

b. Innovation is "change that creates a new dimension of performance." Do we have any opportunities for innovation? If yes, what are they?

c. How well do our internal systems support program performance and innovation? Identify what is strong, what is weak, and what needs to be analyzed.

Internal Systems		Analyze (describe)
Human resource management	☐ Strong ☐ Weak	
Finance/Budget	☐ Strong ☐ Weak	
Development/Fundraising	☐ Strong ☐ Weak	
Marketing, communications, public relations	☐ Strong ☐ Weak	
Quality assurance	☐ Strong ☐ Weak	
Board development	☐ Strong ☐ Weak	
Information technology	☐ Strong ☐ Weak	

Worksheet 4.3:
How Can We Improve
Our Performance?
(Organizational)

a. How do we concentrate our efforts? List each of the organization's programs and identify if it is strong and can produce greater results; if it is weak and in need of improvement; or if it is a candidate for planned abandonment. Explain why.

Programs

1.

☐ Strong/Growth Area
☐ Weak/Needs Improvement
☐ Abandon

2.

☐ Strong/Growth Area
☐ Weak/Needs Improvement
☐ Abandon

3.

☐ Strong/Growth Area
☐ Weak/Needs Improvement
☐ Abandon

4.

☐ Strong/Growth Area
☐ Weak/Needs Improvement
☐ Abandon

5.

☐ Strong/Growth Area
☐ Weak/Needs Improvement
☐ Abandon

b. Innovation is "change that creates a new dimension of performance." Do we have any opportunities for innovation? If yes, what are they?

c. How well do our internal systems support program performance and innovation? Identify what is strong, what is weak, and what needs to be analyzed.

Internal Systems		Analyze (describe)
Human resource management	☐ Strong ☐ Weak	
Finance/Budget	☐ Strong ☐ Weak	
Development/Fundraising	☐ Strong ☐ Weak	
Marketing, communications, public relations	☐ Strong ☐ Weak	
Quality assurance	☐ Strong ☐ Weak	
Board development	☐ Strong ☐ Weak	
Information technology	☐ Strong ☐ Weak	

Question 1:
What Is Our Mission?

Question 2:
Who Is Our Customer?

Question 3:
What Does the
Customer Value?

Question 4:
What Are Our Results?

Question 5: What Is Our Plan?

Worksheet 5.1: What Is Our Mission?

Worksheet 5.2: What Are Our Goals?

Worksheet 5.3: What Is Our Plan to Achieve Results for the Organization?

Worksheet 5.4: How Will We Communicate Our Mission, Plan, and Results?

Question 5:
What Is Our Plan?[8]

Get the Right Things Done

The self-assessment process leads to a plan that is a concise summation of the organization's purpose and future direction. The plan encompasses mission, vision, goals, objectives, action steps, a budget, and appraisal. Now comes the point to affirm or change the mission and set long-range goals. Remember, every mission statement has to reflect three things: opportunities, competence, and commitment. It answers the questions, *What is our purpose? Why do we do what we do? What, in the end, do we want to be remembered for?* The mission transcends today but guides today, informs today. It provides the framework for setting goals and mobilizing the resources of the organization for getting the right things done.

The development and formal adoption of mission and goals are fundamental to effective governance of a nonprofit organization and are primary responsibilities of the board. Therefore, these strategic elements of the plan must be approved by the board.

To further the mission, there must be action today and specific aims for tomorrow. Yet planning is not masterminding the future. Any attempt to do so is foolish; the future is unpredictable. In the face of uncertainties, planning defines the particular place you *want* to be and how you intend to get there. Planning does not substitute facts for judgment nor science for leadership. It recognizes the importance of analysis, courage, experience, intuition—even hunch. It is responsibility rather than technique.

Goals Are Few, Overarching, and Approved by the Board

The most difficult challenge is to agree on the institution's goals—the fundamental long-range direction. Goals are overarching and should be few in number. If you have more than five goals, you have none. You're simply spreading yourself too thin. Goals make it absolutely clear where you will concentrate resources for results—the mark of an organization serious about success. Goals flow from mission, aim the organization where it must go, build on strength, address opportunity, and, taken together, outline your desired future.

An option for the plan is a vision statement picturing a future when the organization's goals are achieved and its mission accomplished. The Leader to Leader Institute's vision is, "to chart the future path for the social sector to become the equal partner of business and government in developing responsible leaders, caring citizens, and a healthy, diverse and inclusive society." I have worked with groups who became intensely motivated by these often idealistic and poetic statements, whereas others say, "Let's not get carried away." If a vision statement—whether a sentence or a page—helps bring the plan to life, by all means include it.

Here is an example of the vision, mission, and goals for an art museum.

Vision	A city where the world's diverse artistic heritage is prized and whose people seek out art to feed their minds and spirits
Mission	To bring art and people together
Goal 1	To conserve the collections and inspire partnerships to seek and acquire exceptional objects
Goal 2	To enable people to discover, enjoy, and understand art through popular and scholarly exhibitions, community education, and publications
Goal 3	To significantly expand the museum's audience and strengthen its impact with new and traditional members
Goal 4	To maintain state-of-the-art facilities, technologies, and operations
Goal 5	To enhance long-term financial security

Building around mission and long-term goals is the only way to integrate shorter-term interests. Then management can always ask, "Is an objective leading us toward our basic long-range goal, or is it going to sidetrack us, divert us, make us lose sight of our aims?" St. Augustine said, "One prays for miracles but works for results." Your plan leads you to work for results. It converts intentions into action.

Objectives Are Measurable, Concrete, and the Responsibility of Management

Objectives are the specific and measurable levels of achievement that move the organization toward its goals. The chief executive officer is responsible for development of objectives and the action steps and detailed budgets that follow. The board must not act at the level of tactical planning, or it interferes with management's vital ability to be flexible in how goals are achieved. When developing and implementing a plan, the board is accountable for mission, goals, and the allocation of resources to results, and for appraising progress and achievement. Management is accountable for objectives, for action steps, for the supporting budget, as well as for demonstrating effective performance.

Five Elements of Effective Plans

Abandonment

The first decision is whether to abandon what does not work, what has never worked—the things that have outlived their usefulness and their capacity to contribute. Ask of any program, system, or customer group, "If we were not committed to this today, would we go into it?" If the answer is no, say, "How can we get out—fast?"

Concentration

Concentration is building on success, strengthening what *does* work. The best rule is to put your efforts into your successes. You will get maximum results. When you have strong performance is the very time to ask, "Can we set an even higher standard?" Concentration is vital, but it's also very risky. You must choose the right concentrations, or—to use a military term—you leave your flanks totally uncovered.

Innovation

You must also look for tomorrow's success, the true innovations, the diversity that stirs the imagination. What are the opportunities, the new conditions, the emerging issues? Do they fit you? Do you really believe in this? But you have to be careful. Before you go into something new, don't say, "This is how we do it." Say, "Let's find out what this requires. What does the customer value? What is the state of the art? How can we make a difference?" Finding answers to these questions is essential.

Risk Taking

Planning always involves decisions on where to take the risks. Some risks you can afford to take—if something goes wrong, it is easily reversible with minor damage.

And some decisions may carry great risk, but you cannot afford *not* to take it. You have to balance the short range with the long. If you are too conservative, you miss the opportunity. If you commit too much too fast, there may not be a long run to worry about. There is no formula for these risk-taking decisions. They are entrepreneurial and uncertain, but they must be made.

Analysis

Finally, in planning it is important to recognize when you do *not* know, when you are not yet sure whether to abandon, concentrate, go into something new, or take a particular risk. Then your objective is to conduct an analysis. Before making the final decision, you study a weak but essential performance area, a challenge on the horizon, the opportunity just beginning to take shape.

Build Understanding and Ownership

The plan begins with a mission. It ends with *action steps* and a *budget.* Action steps establish accountability for objectives—who will do what by when—and the budget commits the resources necessary to implement the plan. To build understanding and ownership for the plan, action steps are developed by the people who will carry them out. Everyone with a role should have the opportunity to give input. This looks incredibly slow. But when the plan is completed, the next day everyone understands it. More people in the organization want the new, are committed to it, are ready to act.

The Self-Assessment Team will prepare the final plan for review by the board. Following presentation and discussion, the board chairman will request approval of the mission, goals, and supporting budget. The chairman may request adoption of a vision statement, if one has been developed, as part of the plan. As soon as approval is given, implementation begins.

Never Really Be Satisfied

This is the last of the self-assessment questions, and your involvement as a participant soon draws to a close. Appraisal will be ongoing. The organization must monitor progress in achieving goals and meeting objectives, and, above all, must measure results in changed lives. You must adjust the plan when conditions change, results are poor, there is a surprise success, or the customer leads you to a place different from where you imagined.

True self-assessment is never finished. Leadership requires constant resharpening, refocusing, never really being satisfied. I encourage you especially to keep asking the question, *What do we want to be remembered for?* It is a question that induces you to renew yourself—and the organization—because it pushes you to see what you can become.

Peter F. Drucker

Figure 1 uses a circular movement to show that evaluation and planning are continuous.

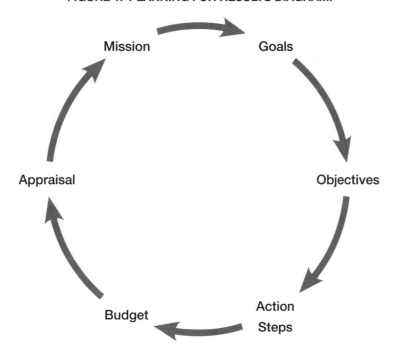

FIGURE 1. PLANNING FOR RESULTS DIAGRAM.

Mission is essential to social sector planning. The mission answers the questions, What is our reason for being? Why do we do what we do? For what, in the end, do we want to be remembered? From the mission flow goals that set the organization's fundamental long-range direction and, together, outline its desired future. Objectives are specific and measurable levels of achievement. Action steps are the detailed plans and activities to meet the objectives; the budget commits necessary resources; and appraisal demonstrates whether objectives are met and results achieved.

Worksheet 5.1:
What Is Our Mission?
(Workshop)

a. The vision is a picture of the organization's desired future. If the organization would like to develop a vision, what is it?

b. The mission answers the questions, What is our reason for being? Does the mission need to be revisited? (Refer to Worksheet 1.2.)

☐ Yes   ☐ No

c. What is our mission?

Worksheet 5.1:
What Is Our Mission?
(Organizational)

a. The vision is a picture of the organization's desired future. If the organization would like to develop a vision, what is it?

b. The mission answers the questions, What is our reason for being? Does the mission need to be revisited? (Refer to Worksheet 1.2.)

　　　☐ Yes　　☐ No

c. What is our mission?

Goals are a set of three to five aims that set the organization's fundamental, long-range direction.

What are our goals?

1.

2.

3.

4.

5.

Worksheet 5.2:
What Are Our Goals?
(Organizational)

Goals are a set of three to five aims that set the organization's fundamental, long-range direction.

What are our goals?

1.

2.

3.

4.

5.

Worksheet 5.3:
What Is Our Plan to Achieve
Results for the Organization?
(Workshop)

The mission and goals are approved by the board of directors before the plan is developed. This worksheet serves as a template to help the organization prepare the plan. To better understand the elements of the plan, refer to Figure 1 on page 83.

Goals	Objectives (Measurable)	Action Steps (Measurable)	Budget Implications (Measurable)	Target Date (Completion)	Staffing (Support Needed)
1.					
2.					
3.					

The Five Most Important Questions Self-Assessment Tool, Participant Workbook, Third Edition. Copyright © 2010 by Leader to Leader Institute. Reproduced by permission of Jossey-Bass, an Imprint of Wiley.

Worksheet 5.3:
What Is Our Plan to Achieve
Results for the Organization? (cont'd)
(Workshop)

Goals	Objectives (Measurable)	Action Steps (Measurable)	Budget Implications (Measurable)	Target Date (Completion)	Staffing (Support Needed)
4.					
5.					

Worksheet 5.3:
What Is Our Plan to Achieve
Results for the Organization?
(Organizational)

The mission and goals are approved by the board of directors before the plan is developed. This worksheet serves as a template to help the organization prepare the plan. To better understand the elements of the plan, refer to Figure 1 on page 83.

Goals	Objectives (Measurable)	Action Steps (Measurable)	Budget Implications (Measurable)	Target Date (Completion)	Staffing (Support Needed)
1.					
2.					
3.					

The Five Most Important Questions Self-Assessment Tool, Participant Workbook, Third Edition. Copyright © 2010 by Leader to Leader Institute. Reproduced by permission of Jossey-Bass, an Imprint of Wiley.

Worksheet 5.3: What Is Our Plan to Achieve Results for the Organization? (cont'd) (Organizational)

Goals	Objectives (Measurable)	Action Steps (Measurable)	Budget Implications (Measurable)	Target Date (Completion)	Staffing (Support Needed)
4.					
5.					

The Five Most Important Questions Self-Assessment Tool, Participant Workbook, Third Edition. Copyright © 2010 by Leader to Leader Institute. Reproduced by permission of Jossey-Bass, an Imprint of Wiley.

Worksheet 5.4:
How Will We Communicate Our Mission, Plan, and Results?
(Workshop)

How will we communicate our mission, plan, and results to our primary and supporting customers?

How will we communicate our mission, plan, and results to our primary and supporting customers?

Afterword

Effective Implementation of the Plan[9]

Work doesn't get done by a magnificent statement of policy. Work is only done when it's done. Done by people. By people who are properly informed, assigned, and equipped. People with a deadline. People who are developed and evaluated. The best plan is *only* a plan—a set of good intentions—unless there is communication, action, appraisal, and the continuous reallocation of the organization's resources to getting results. The immediate test of a plan is whether leadership actually commits resources to its implementation. Unless such commitment is made, there are only promises and hopes—but no plan.

Communication, Development of People, and Performance

The nonprofit organization must be information-based. Information must flow from the individuals doing the work to the board and management, and it must flow back as well. In a national voluntary organization, the day after the board approved the organization's plan, the chairman was off on a round of visits to local chapters. At each stop she met with leaders and gave speeches focused on vision, mission, goals, and how the local chapter could contribute to results. She answered question after question from individual members and encouraged them to communicate their experience and observations directly to national leadership as time went on. Simultaneously, the executive director held meetings with staff; confirmed new assignments; and led discussion on objectives, action steps, and how progress and achievement would be appraised. The board chairman and chief executive immediately demonstrated their commitment to the plan and set the stage for ongoing communication.

Management emphasis should always be on performance. But, especially for a nonprofit organization, it must also be on developing people. Staff and volunteers require clear assignments that tap their strengths and allow them—through training, encouragement, and the right challenges—to expand these strengths. They need frequent and open opportunities to review team and individual performance. They need leaders and managers who sit down and say, "This is what you and I committed ourselves to. How have we done? What should we do to further your growth?" The guideline is, if people try, work with them. Look for a different way they can contribute. But if a person cannot perform, another assignment should be considered. The alternative is that all those who have to work with the person lose their capacity to contribute. Without management resolve in these difficult situations, the plan becomes hollow.

Appraisal Is All Important

What we measure and how we measure it determines what will be considered relevant and thereby determines not just what we see but what we—and others—do. Monitoring should be built in early, involve people at all levels of the organization, and give leadership the ability to quickly take corrective action or move to build on success. There must be systematic feedback—a way of self-control from events back to planning.

Your plan commits present resources to the uncertainties of the future. This, according to elementary probability mathematics, means some decisions will prove to be wrong. Adjusting them requires two things: first, that you think through alternatives ahead of time so that you have something to fall back on, and second, that you build into the plan the responsibility for bailing it out instead of arguing about who made what mistakes.

When a new tactic or action doesn't seem to be working, the rule is, "If at first you don't succeed, try once more." Stop and ask what has been learned. Try to improve the strategy, to change it, and to make another major effort. Maybe, although I am reluctant to encourage it, you should make a third effort. After that, go to work where the results are.

Appraisal should not focus on flaws and mistakes at the expense of achievement. There is a tendency to devote the most time to problem solving, to pour more and more into rescuing a failure. When you have results, communicate them, give recognition where it is due, and reward effectiveness. Take time to analyze what has gone *right,* how even better results might be achieved, how success in one area can be translated to others.

At the same time, bear in mind that no success is forever. It is far more difficult to abandon yesterday's success than it is to reappraise failure. Success breeds its own hubris. It creates emotional attachment, habits of mind and action, and, above all, false self-confidence. A success that has outlived its usefulness—and today this happens very quickly—may, in the end, be more damaging than failure.

Mission Is the Star to Steer By

A plan is a framework, not a formula. When conditions change, when complex decisions must be made, first ask, "What will further the mission?" Then look to goals, to what results should and *could* be. The greatest mistake when implementing a plan is to allow objectives to become a straitjacket; commitment to mission and goals is long term, but one always makes compromises on tactics.

I know of a public health organization that was approached by a school system asking for a partnership, a means for that public health organization to take a prevention program directly into the classroom and reach children—the primary customers—quickly and in great numbers. They struggled over the opportunity because "it wasn't in the plan," and their people were already working on a different approach. It took open minds and managerial agility to change direction, to take the entrepreneurial risk and abandon an objective mid-course in favor of a more effective one.

My hope, as you complete this formal process, is that you do not stop with "what is in the plan" but make true self-assessment an ongoing practice. This means constant scanning of the environment, continual learning from the customer. It means appraisal, countless small adjustments, and the courage to make major change. True self-assessment creates, through dedication and hard work, that flow of knowledge throughout the organization that strengthens judgment, renews leadership, and inspires vision. It is the foundation of excellence in performance.

Peter F. Drucker

Glossary of Terms

ACTION STEPS Detailed plans and activities that meet an organization's objectives.

APPRAISAL Process for monitoring progress in meeting objectives and achieving results; point at which the action steps for meeting objectives may be modified on the basis of experience or changed conditions.

BUDGET The commitment of resources necessary to implement plans—the financial expression of a particular plan of work.

CONCENTRATION Strengthening what works. The organization focuses on the programs and activities that contribute to achieving the right results.

CONSTRUCTIVE DISSENT Using dissent or disagreement as an opportunity to "[create] understanding and mutual respect."[10]

CUSTOMER VALUE That which satisfies customers' needs (physical and psychological well-being), wants (where, when, and how service or product is provided), and aspirations (desired future results).

CUSTOMERS Those who must be satisfied in order for the organization to achieve results. The *primary customer* is the person whose life is changed through the organization's work. *Supporting customers* are volunteers, members, partners, funders, referral sources, staff, and others who must be satisfied in order for the organization to achieve results.

DEPTH INTERVIEWS One-on-one interviews used to highlight the insights of a select group of individuals inside the organization. Interview findings provide a touchstone for facilitated discussion and decision making.

ENVIRONMENTAL SCAN To find and identify change . . . by examining the sources and direction of change as they become evident through [research] media, publications, and individual observation and experience.[11]

GOALS A set of three to five aims that set the organization's fundamental, future direction.

INNOVATION Change that creates a new dimension of performance.[12]

INTERNAL DATA Summarized information regarding the history, present status, and performance of the organization.

LEADERSHIP TEAM The chairman of the board and the chief executive officer of the organization. Both lead organizational self-assessment.

MISSION The organization's reason for being, its purpose. Says what, in the end, the organization wants to be remembered for.

OBJECTIVES Specific and measurable levels of achievement that move an organization toward its goals.

PLAN A concise summation of the organization's purpose and future direction. The plan encompasses vision, mission, goals, objectives, action steps, a budget, and appraisal.[13]

PLANNED ABANDONMENT Removing or stopping programs and activities that are decreasing in relevance or not producing adequate results.

QUALITATIVE MEASURES Address the depth and breadth of change within a particular context. The measures begin with specific observations; build toward patterns; and tell a subtle, individualized story.[14]

QUANTITATIVE MEASURES Use definitive standards. The measures begin with categories and expectations and tell an objective story.[15]

RESULTS The organization's bottom line. Defined in changed lives—behavior, circumstances, health, hopes, competence, or capacity. Results are always outside the organization.

TREND A statement of the direction of change.[16]

VISION A picture of the organization's desired future when the organization's goals are achieved and its mission accomplished.

Notes

1. *The Drucker Foundation Self-Assessment Tool: Participant Workbook,* Revised Edition (San Francisco: Jossey-Bass, 1999), pp. 3–6.

2. 1999 *Participant Workbook,* pp. 14–16.

3. *The Five Most Important Questions You Will Ever Ask About Your Nonprofit Organization: Participant's Workbook* (San Francisco: Jossey-Bass, 1993), p. 13.

4. 1999 *Participant Workbook,* p. 16.

5. 1999 *Participant Workbook,* pp. 22–24.

6. 1999 *Participant Workbook,* pp. 32–34.

7. 1999 *Participant Workbook,* pp. 40–44.

8. 1999 *Participant Workbook,* pp. 52–56.

9. 1999 *Participant Workbook,* pp. 59–61.

10. Peter F. Drucker, *Managing the Nonprofit Organization: Principles and Practices* (New York: HarperCollins, 1990), p. 125.

11. James G. Dalton, Jennifer Jarratt, and John B. Mahaffie, *From Scan to Plan: Integrating Trends into the Strategy-Making Process: Executive Summary* (Washington, D.C.: Foundation of the American Society of Association Executives, 2003), p. 12.

12. Peter F. Drucker, *Innovation and Entrepreneurship, Practice and Principles* (New York: Harper & Row, 1985).

13. 1999 *Participant Workbook,* p. 52.

14. 1999 *Participant Workbook,* p. 41.

15. 1999 *Participant Workbook,* p. 41.

16. Dalton, Jarratt, and Mahaffie, *From Scan to Plan,* p. 4.

About Frances Hesselbein

Frances Hesselbein is the president and CEO of the Leader to Leader Institute (formerly the Peter F. Drucker Foundation for Nonprofit Management) and its founding president. In 1998, Mrs. Hesselbein was awarded the Presidential Medal of Freedom, the highest civilian honor in the United States of America. The award recognized her leadership as CEO of Girl Scouts of the U.S.A. from 1976–1990, her role as the founding president of the Drucker Foundation, and her service as a pioneer for women, volunteerism, diversity, and opportunity. President George H. W. Bush appointed her to two Presidential commissions on national and community service.

In 2009, Mrs. Hesselbein was appointed the *Class of 1951 Chair for the Study of Leadership* at the United States Military Academy at West Point's Department of Behavioral Sciences and Leadership. She is the first woman and first non-graduate to serve in this chair. Also in 2009, the University of Pittsburgh initiated *The Hesselbein Global Academy for Student Leadership and Civic Engagement.* The Academy aims to develop a cadre of experienced, ethical leaders equipped to address critical issues throughout the world.

Mrs. Hesselbein serves on many nonprofit and corporate boards, including Mutual of America Life Insurance Company; Bright China Social Fund; American Express Philanthropy; the Center for Social Initiative, Harvard Business School; the Hauser Center for Nonprofit Management, Harvard Kennedy School; the Graduate School of International Relations and Pacific Studies, University of California, San Diego; and the Alliance Advisory Council for the Center for Creative Leadership. She was the Chairman of Volunteers of America from 2002–2006.

Mrs. Hesselbein was duly honored with a Lifetime Award for her exceptional work as former CEO of Girl Scouts of the U.S.A. and her continued commitment to developing leaders of all ages. She was inducted into the Enterprising Women Hall of Fame at the 7th Annual Enterprising Women of the Year Awards Celebration. She is the recipient of twenty honorary doctoral degrees.

In 2008, Mrs. Hesselbein was presented with the International Leadership Association's Lifetime Achievement Award and the Tempo International Leadership Award. In this same year, she was named a Senior Leader at the United States Military

Academy National Conference on Ethics in America. In 2007, Mrs. Hesselbein was awarded the John F. Kennedy Memorial Fellowship by Fulbright New Zealand. In 2003, she was the first recipient of the Dwight D. Eisenhower National Security Award.

Mrs. Hesselbein is editor-in-chief of the award-winning quarterly journal *Leader to Leader*, and a coeditor of a book of the same name. She is the author of *Hesselbein on Leadership* and with General Eric K. Shinseki, introduced *Be*Know*Do: Leadership the Army Way*. Mrs. Hesselbein is the coeditor of 27 books in 29 languages.

Acknowledgments

We are deeply grateful to the leaders, facilitators, and organizations that have contributed their time, inquisitiveness, and expertise to the third edition of *The Five Most Important Questions Self-Assessment Tool*. Over one hundred leaders representing more than seventy organizations helped field test the *Tool*.

We thank the leaders and facilitators who have worked tirelessly to bring Peter Drucker's *Self-Assessment Tool* to the social sector. We would like to thank Constance Rossum for her assistance in developing the first edition and Gary Stern for assisting in developing the second edition. Among the many individuals who helped shape the third edition are Derek Bell, Theresa Berenato, Dee Ann Boyd, Risa Cohn, Cathy Crosky, Susan Diamond, Carla Grantham, Justine Green, Lawrence Greenspan, Kathy Long Holland, Lee Igel, Irv Katz, Patricia Lewis, Matthew MacPherson, Michael Millar, Maria Carpenter Ort, Peggy Morrison Outon, Katherina Rosqueta, Doug Schallau, Kevin S. Smith, Iain Somerville, Bonita and Mark Thompson, Robert Clifford Uerz, and Tamara Woodbury.

Special thanks go to Frances Hesselbein for her guidance and her commitment to the social sector and performance excellence; she has been a tireless champion for Peter Drucker's work and for bringing The Five Most Important Questions to the social sector. Our appreciation goes to Jesse Wiley, our editorial partner at Jossey-Bass/Wiley, as well as to Susan Rachmeler and Nina Kreiden, who helped develop and produce the publications there. We thank Cathey Brown and Claire Walden for their work developing, editing, and field testing this revised edition.

We would like to thank the Bright China Social Fund and the Buford Foundation for their generosity in making this edition of the *Tool* possible. We also thank the American Management Association and the Women Presidents' Organization for supporting The Five Most Important Questions workshops.

Our final thanks go to Peter F. Drucker for his dedication to the effective organization, for his contributions to management literature and practices, and for his support and contributions to the social sector. Without him, his wisdom and his passion, Leader to Leader would not exist and publishing these materials would not be possible.

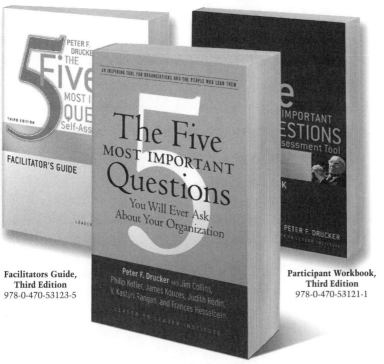